AMERICA: FUBAR!

Democracy In America?
Volume IV

Lucy Nalangu

James Sawers

* Photo: Professor Lucy Nalangu, PhD, CBE

** Some of the things mentioned in this book have to do with current events, the outcomes of which have yet to be determined, as of date of publishing.

***A special thanks to Dr. Mark Sharp for his title suggestions for this book.

This Fine Book Belongs To:

Books of poetry by James Sawers

Nothing Series:

Nothing Works 2nd ED
Meditations on Aikido,
Buddhism, the Tao, Zen, and
other inconsequential things...
Nothing Special: Vol II
Nothing Matters: Vol III
Nothing Exists; Vol IV
Nothing Flows Vol. V

War Series:

Words of War 2nd ed.
Warm Beer Is Not Cool
Go Tell the Crows
Common Blood
Military Maxims*
Military Maxims II*
The Hard Way
(Upcoming)

Color Series: 2nd ed.

Red
Lust Is a Monster
Poems of Life, Love, and Loss

Green
The Other Monster

Blue
The Indigo Moments of Life

Politics

Trumpets -
Poetic Observations on a Presidency
Are You a Nutjob?
The Cockwomble President

Democracy in America? Series

American Judgement*
In Search of Value*
Power & State*
America: FUBAR*

Life Series/Standalone

In the Shadows of the Ordinary
Too Deep for Tears
Rainy Nights in Chicago
Silent Love
She Wears the Wind
Accidental Gods
The Colors of Time
Strange Thoughts
Cold Warmth
Kitchen Sink Poetry
Olympus Mons or Bust!
Whispers
Scottish Haiku
Shared Thoughts
Obvious Thoughts
One Life
Just South of Midnight
Broken Things

Humanity Interstellar Series

Humanity Interstellar
The Way of the Vessel*
The Way of the Vessel II*
Humanity Interstellar II
(Upcoming)

<u>Religion/Mysticism</u>

Non-Poetry

AMERICA: FUBAR!

x

Otpor Productions

DEMOCRACY IN AMERICA? SERIES
Volume IV

Nothing-Werks, Inc.
nothingwerks42@gmail.com

America: FUBAR!

First Printing July, 2024
ISBN: 9798332281006

FUBAR!

We've all heard the term
And perhaps thought it applied
To a situation close to us:
Fucked Up Beyond All Recognition!

And perhaps it did
But this term, this feeling
Is universal and everyone
Has had a big YEAH!
When their own FUBAR! arrived

But when it becomes chronic
When FUBAR! becomes SNAFU:
Situation Normal All Fucked UP
Then it is truly a WTF time!

~ Tristan Graeme Ash

We therefore should not console ourselves by thinking that the barbarians are still a long way off. Some peoples may let the torch be snatched from their hands, but others stamp it out themselves.

~ Alexis de Tocqueville

FUBAR

*Before mass leaders seize the power to fit reality to
their lies, their propaganda is marked by extreme
contempt for facts as such.*
~ Hannah Arendt

*It is easier for the world to accept a
simple lie than a complex truth.*
~ Alexis de Tocqueville

*A president cannot defend a nation if he
is not held accountable to its laws.*
~ DaShanne Stokes

*A prude thinks that his own rules of
propriety are natural laws.*
~ Robert A. Heinlein

*As soon as any man says of the affairs of the State
'What does it matter to me?' the State
may be given up for lost.*
~ Jean-Jacques Rousseau

*'There is more than one kind of freedom,'
said Aunt Lydia. 'Freedom to and freedom from.
In the days of anarchy, it was freedom to. Now you are
being given freedom from. Don't underrate it.'*
~ Margaret Atwood

A State for one man is no State at all.
~ Sophocles

*Freedom is the freedom to say that two
plus two make four.*
~ George Orwell

Contents

OVERVIEW

Lucy Nalangu is a Professor of Law, History & Moral Philosophy, PhD, CBE. She is a teacher, writer, social activist, social scientist, and political philosopher, formerly Professor of Law, History & Moral Philosophy at the University of Nairobi, previously taught at the University of Oxford, UK, and at Harvard University, US. Currently, she is a freelance researcher, professional writer, commentator, and consultant.

This volume is a compilation (with permission) of her thoughts, opinions, and ideas, extracted from her published works, her unpublished manuscripts, and personal conversations.

As with Alexis de Tocqueville, almost two centuries before her, Professor Nalangu brings an outsider view on the happenings in the United States, perhaps more objective than native-born.

She also shares the same belief of Tocqueville, that the ongoing movement toward democracy in the West, and perhaps the entire world, is one of the greatest overriding themes in history.

That the drive towards equality for all is one of the most important political and social ideas human civilization has brought forth.

She understands and celebrates the sometimes-sensitive balance that can occur between liberty and equality, the individual, and the community-at-large.

She believes that Democracy cannot be taken for granted, but must be fought for and protected for the value it brings to Humanity and to its future promise.

But there needs to be a constant reminder, that the power of the State, in a Democracy, is derived from the people. Many times, this is so easy to forget, by the State as well as by the people.

The writings herein attempt to straddle the line between the concrete mundane, offering opinions, insights, and possible courses of practical, realistic appraisal and action applicable to the here-and-now, to a type of philosophical speculation that tries to avoid extravagant overstatement.

However, this volume in the *Democracy in America?* series, takes a critical close look at the current state of democracy in America.

Words with an asterisk* after them will be found in the DEFINITION section at the back of the book, along with others that may help in understanding the context in which certain words and concepts are used.

FUBAR?

SECRET CARPENTERS

They toiled hard through the ages
Unknown to each other
Yet sharing a common goal
Sharing common beliefs
Creating secret power bases
Working towards their secret agenda
Raising a timber here, one there
Building their great, secret edifice
With long patience and skill
Now they are out in the open
Their orange champion babbling on
Their agenda no longer secret
The subjugation of women
And all '*inferior*' peoples
Those secret carpenters
From the highest offices
To the thugs marching in the streets
TIKI torches held high
So proud of the new slave pens
Being erected, the barbed wire
Surrounding the soul of the nation
Who has the axe of justice?
Who has the purifying fire?
Who has the termites?

~ Elizabeth Rutherglen

QUOTES & NOTES

Republican politicians have taken up the mantle of former totalitarian regimes in their complete acceptance of the idea that politics is a game of cheating, domestically and internationally. They throw out absurd lies, that no rational person would take seriously, and before the dust settles, throw out more and more. Politics has taken on the veneer of war, where cheating, lying, become mere tactics, and are all totally acceptable as long as it leads to victory. The American political system or public has not yet consciously caught up to this yet. They need to.

For some people the outrageousness of an idea does not hinder its belief.

Keep in mind, that for many MAGA supporters, control of the State is only a means to an end. For some, it is about establishing their Christian Fascist State, though, of course, they would not characterize it that way. For others, it is just for the accumulation of power and what they could do with it. Either way, any form of effective governance is at least secondary, perhaps not even that.

The pursuit and actualization of their own interests is primary, regardless of the negative effects this may have on the majority of people, or to the country* as a whole.

Many wannabe dictators* have the rare ability to form a bond with some people such that these people feel a trust and commonality between them where none actually exits. That 'mutual' loyalty that they feel is entirely one-sided. When they finally march to the barricades, they will be alone.

Totalitarian regimes, while usually based on absurdity, tell lies with no actual basis in reality. Once in power, and to maintain power, it turns those same lies into actuality by acting as if they real.

Their lies are no longer questionable as they are now lived by the people each and every day, with very real consequences. The self-fulfilling logic is inescapable and unending.

The actual reality of Trump speeches (rants?) is not based on logic or rationality. But for the people who listen and he reaches, he voices a reality that they believe exists in their lives. The only way to counter this reckless indifference to truth is with a stronger argument, but not one based on logic, charts, figures, etc., but one with an even stronger emotional appeal. Truth has its own emotional resonance.

If Trump and his allies actually gain power, they will construct a governmental organization based on their various, sometimes competing, lies.

This organizational structure will not be based on objective reality, but only the reality of the organization itself.

The outside world will look on in wonder and perplexity as the most powerful nation in the world self-destructs, fearful it will take them with it.*

Many of the MAGA-right do not believe in democracy, in the equality of all people. Their version of 'equality' is an equality of 'nature'. Their nature is superior to all others, certainly not equal. Only within their own kind is any type of 'equality' possible. But even here, there is always the uber-equal.

The totalitarian mindset is binary. It is us vs them. Them being the enemy. And once in power, the enemy is shown no quarter.

Unfortunately, many in the totalitarian camp do not see this full picture. They think that they can support a wannabe dictator, vote for him and his 'policies' (he has none beyond the attainment and accumulation of power), yet live a normal life, meld back in with their neighbours, and partake in the normal society they have now betrayed.

But the more power this seeker-of-power accumulates, the less he needs them, those blind supporters, till finally, they themselves become swept away in totalitarian paranoia.

The inner ranks of a totalitarian regime have no patience, respect, or need for masses of true believers, those gullible, ignorant, and stupid enough to put them in power.

Whether you are pro-left or pro-right, or somewhere in the middle, it does not matter, as long as you are pro-democracy.

The Republican Party's continuous criticism and assault on the FBI and the Department of Justice for their apparent corruption and lack of diligence in pursuing charges and criminal indictments against certain Democrats and their allies, is only a poorly disguised charade.

The Republicans, themselves, cannot wait to take over power sufficient to weaponize all the powers of these organizations against their 'enemies'. It would be only a matter of time before they attempt to use the military or police in a like fashion.

It is obvious that the mass of Trump supporters follows him for the simplicity of his message: US against THEM. Gone are the confusing nuances of modern life in a pluralistic society. The clarity of simplistic thinking for a lot of people is a powerful attractor and motivator.

For once, conspiracy theorists are correct, there is an inner circle that is attempting to control and manipulate reality, the reality of their lives.

But this inner circle is composed of power hungry, usually insane people, whose only true goal is power.

They have no hidden agenda beyond that. No grand scheme to form a 'paradise' on earth. No, they just want power. If necessary, they will bring the world down around them, and us, in this pursuit.

When a totalitarian movement is on the rise, and takes power, the existing laws of the land are extinguished. The only law a totalitarian power accepts, and lives by, is the 'Law of Killing'.

All the lies the MAGA-right express almost daily, are not to hide a secret. Their goals are clearly expressed, just no one sufficiently believes them.

Their stated goals are to gain power to implement their agendas. Whether it is some sort of Christian Nationalism, or the Republican wet-dream of a return to some sort of an Ayn Rand style of laissez-faire capitalist Darwinism.

The lies are used as a tool, as a clan or tribal ritual, that they use to contemptuously laugh at the gullible masses.

They proudly stand there in their lies, using them to separate themselves, their lying tribe, from the fools who listen to them. Their lies are their truths.

The road to insanity is not made by rational choice.

Many Trump supporters know that each time he speaks, they recognize he is lying. But this is okay, they think he is lying for them. If lying to others gets them into power, that can only be a good thing. And if anyone actually believes him, they deserve what they get for being so stupid and gullible. They, themselves, know better, and will, of course, be exempt from the consequences.

The powerful of the far-right, filter down through their ranks, and finally to the masses, tactical lies that constantly change. These lies are for a public that still thinks and operates as if truth matters, and therefore, seeks it out. But eventually lies and truth meld together such that people become contemptuous of 'truth' and see it as having no real function in their lives.

In totalitarian rule, the normal laws of the land, the rule of law everyone is usually expected and obliged to live under, are bypassed. New laws, such as they stand, are enforced without first outlining what exactly they are. People are expected to obey laws that do not exist. Yet, the consequences of disobedience are very real.

The overall totalitarian ideology that drove it to power are supposed to be all the direction and guidance needed. Typical legal and social institutions crumble as they now have no standing, function, or power.

Chaos rules the land. For those in power, this is a good thing as people, now rootless, cannot organize or protest, as they now stand alone. At least under a dictatorship, there is a target, and usually, a dictator maintains, and uses the very legal and social structures he inherited, to enforce and channel his power.

In a totalitarian regime instead, we have an amorphous movement that shifts, yet hides in plain sight, as everyone, without exception, is now part of it, whether they want to be or not.

⬡ *When Trump and his MAGA allies take an oath to protect and uphold the Constitution of the United States, they are obviously lying. All their prior actions indicate this. Unless taking this oath has a bite for non-compliance, such people will continue to lie their way into power.*

But even before they have reached this point and taken this oath, they have shown beforehand their true intentions. So, the standards for taking and holding public office needs to be clearly established and enforced.

The American body politic needs to finally take seriously this ongoing, looming threat to American democracy, and by extension, the other democracies of the world.

⬡ *A movement based on constant expansion has within it, its own death.*

Totalitarianism can be likened to a disease. It needs no outside laws to govern people because the 'laws' are already inherent in the people. Therefore, no external laws are required.*

People automatically conform to the requirements of the disease. People are merely carriers. That is their function. The disease knows, in its unfolding, what is best.

To fight it would go against a basic law of nature. So, any police action taken against the people, is to protect the disease, to enhance the infection. Plus, the disease looks good on the people so infected.

Blind conceit, blind insanity, is what drives a wannabe dictator to power, and what also, ultimately brings him down.

The main-street media needs to stop acting surprised that Trump and his allies lie all the time. They need to stop having televised round-tables of talking heads analyzing this and that lie, looking for true meaning and intent. They will find none. The lies are true lies.

They need to stop giving these lies airtime. All they are doing is repeating these lies and giving them power in the simple fact of acknowledging them. Stop it.

The Media has a role in American society besides trying to get good ratings. Focus on this role, and fulfill it. Otherwise, there will come a time in America when all you will do is sit in front of a camera and read the 'news' provided by nameless men in far-away offices, and listened to by miserable masses devoid of interest or hope.

The 'total' quality of totalitarianism betrays its intent. Its intent is aspirational in that it is actually a movement, global in its scope. It only exists to dominate all others. If it says otherwise it is lying. But lies are just one of its many tools.

In a totalitarian regime, the regime's greatest fear is not the enemy 'outside', but within its own ranks, within its own people.

They take a resistant individual down deep into their secret catacombs. There they do diabolical things to this non-believer, this naysayer. They take him apart physically, emotionally, and mentally, till finally they ask him: 'What do you believe?'

They have their own Grand Inquisitor whose task is to determine if this person is finally the One. The One who sees through all their lies and fabrications, whose faith trumps their power. This search for the One is never-ending.

Each victim is asked the same question: 'What do you believe?' All so far, have answered 'correctly' and then have been quietly disappeared.

Still, their search continues, for they know that somewhere out there is an unrequited, unrepentant, non-believer, and they are determined to find that person.

What happens when a totalitarian power wins? When it has secured its borders and now has also gained total global domination? That its one and only operating philosophy has been successful, what does it do?

It slowly dies. Its own concept of some kind of internal perpetual revolution cannot keep enough inner dynamism alive, as it eats itself. Eventually, it runs out of victims.

In the dying it can and will kill all the people it can, and the whole planet if it thinks it needs to and has the power.

It has created and lived in a fictional world for so long, facts are immaterial, including the fact of global death. The power-elite always think they are immune, even as they die too, almost willing victims to their own insanity.

The inner-circle followers of a 'Great Leader' know he is not infallible, even if that is the image publicly displayed and portrayed. But individually, they think they are.

Lies have power, yes. But only if believed by enough people. Lies by themselves are like moths fluttering before the flame of truth. They are helpless, useless, powerless, and if they get too close, will just burn away. Reality is truth. It can be denied, ignored, but it will never go away. It waits as patiently as circumstances allow, ready for eventual acknowledgement, one way or another.

In a totalitarian world, failure is not recognized. The country as a whole could be imploding right in front of its leaders and people, and it would be denied, as true reality is always denied if it contradicts, and in defence of its operating ideology. This black-hole of failure, sucking in everything around it, will strike out at anything in its dying way, including its own people.

In totalitarian regimes, the ultimate victory of lie and fiction over truth and reality is of course, up to the people. The elite, the so-called 'Great Leader', are all helpless without the people. After all, the elites are just parasites feeding off the masses. But the masses have to know and understand this for them to finally resist.

The alternative of not resisting is to literally be crushed physically, mentally, and emotionally such that the masses become helpless drones they, the elite, can continue to feed off of. Make no mistake, they will bleed you dry.

In a totalitarian regime, the only freedom left for the individual is suicide. So, when you hear the leaders of such a regime extoll the 'freedom' of its people, you have to wonder.

A totalitarian regime garners power, gathers power unto itself, in preparation for its direct confrontation with Reality. It needs all the power it can collect for Reality is powerful. Reality is Nature's default setting.

Totalitarianism attempts to create a separate reality. It needs all the power it can get to do this, for its reality is fictitious, it is fake, its foundation is based on lies, hence, basically weak. If it slacked off in the slightest, True Reality would breach its ramparts and destroy it.

Despite the modern difficulty of discerning truth from fiction in today's internet world, truth is still the enemy of lies, the final antiseptic that lies are so afraid of, for one-on-one, lies have no chance. Whatever people may believe, truth has its own reality where lies cannot exist.

Look to the ideology of the MAGA-right. What do they believe? Once in power, how would their beliefs become actualized in the real world?

Some outcomes have already been realized. The overturning of Roe v. Wade, for instance, and the cascade of similar anti-choice legislations in various states – MAGA dominated states. Also, the beginning of the dismantling of the 'administrative state' (which some mistakenly believe is a victory over 'big government' – which it is not. See Definitions in back of book for a brief definition of the 'administrative state'). The criminalization of the homeless and immigrants. Isolationism tendencies in a world looking, needing, American leadership.

It goes on and on. These are not all isolated incidents, but direct, connected, outcomes of the MAGA-right (and their financial backers) ideology. Follow their logic. It will require thought, perhaps some research.

In an interdependent political, financial, ecological world system, how will all this play out? How will this be good for America? For the planet? The logic of their belief system does not take actual, real *people into account – a ten-year old rape victim not allowed to terminate a forced pregnancy, must escape to another state* to terminate this pregnancy. Sounds like a dystopian movie! Their so-called 'sanctity of life' argument is killing American women all across the country.*

Other examples are all over the news. The FDA, the EPA, and other government agencies not allowed to use science and their subject-matter expertise, under the law, to create rules and regulations to help guide and safeguard the American public.

But this is good, right? Less 'interference' from 'Big Brother'. But think it through to how actual people are affected – you, your family, your friends and neighbours. The logic of their ideology eats up real people. It is inherent in its blind premise.

Dictators dress their ideologies in fancy dress: class struggle; pure race struggle; conspiracy struggle; religious struggle, etc., but underneath those frills and pretty petticoats, you will find pure hatred, pure fear, pure lust, pure insanity.

In a democracy, a single individual can say 'No'. This is a right, sometimes a duty and obligation. In a totalitarian regime, while a 'No' can equate to a death sentence, it is still the one word such power is most afraid of. For the implications of a single 'No' has the power to topple a regime.

True believers are sometimes surprised that when they finally, truly achieve ultimate domination, when their beliefs fall away because they are no longer needed, and only pure power remains, they easily lose what humanity they may have left.

Homo sapiens – *wise human. Self-named, of course. Because looking at the history of Humanity, maybe not so wise.*

Sure, Humanity has accomplished some great things in its short existence on this planet, but its lasting, perhaps final legacy, will be its inability to self-govern, and its possible total destruction of most life on earth, including its own.

Would another intelligent species call us: Homo sapiens? *Perhaps not.*

The lust, the drive for power is free from ideological content. There might be an organizing principal that creates structure around which everything operates, but that is just a tool, for even that may change if necessary if it fails in its purpose. Power is the goal.

Truth and reality are not of great concern to totalitarian regimes. The only concern is victory. Creating lies and fictional realities is part of their method for achieving victory. These lies and fictions supersede everything else.

But even if these lies and fictions do eventually bring success and power, such a regime can never stop dancing on this false quicksand of a manufactured reality. It cannot help but eventually destroy itself, destroying everything it touches, trying to maintain its own fictions.

But internal collapse is preordained. It is only a matter of how much damage is done to the people and to the world, before this collapse occurs.

Whatever ideology a so-called 'Great Leader' and his inner-circle have espoused, they are lying. It cannot ever be overstated that their only allegiance, their only god, is power.

In a totalitarian regime, the role of the police has become much simpler: everyone is guilty. Mass purges, so common in totalitarian states, seem to follow the ancient Chinese system of collective responsibility and punishment for a 'crime'. Under that system, when a criminal is sentenced to death, all other family members were also sentenced to death. This included the wife's family or siblings' families. This so-called 'nine familial exterminations', *involved the execution of all relatives of an individual, which were categorized into nine groups, a system of degrees of responsibility.*

The killing of extended family members could proceed by varying degrees, nine degrees considered extreme. What this means is that anyone connected by blood, even faintly, as degrees enlarge, is killed for the crime the original individual may have done.

The totalitarian state has gone even further. The connections to the original 'criminal' are no longer just determined by blood-line, but includes anyone even remotely connected, even complete strangers, who might have crossed paths with someone known to someone, known to.... It goes on and on, with only some obscure, tenuous link back to the original nexus.

Countless people can be swept up in such purges, the end result being that even the memories of people's former existence is wiped out. There is no one left alive to remember. This is the intent.

In a totalitarian regime, an 'enemy of the state' is not determined by any action taken, or even planned, by said enemy, no. This status is determined by the state, using whatever pretext is useful at the time.

 Life in a totalitarian state can be likened to life in the world of the movie Minority Report. *A citizen is arrested and punished, not for anything done, but for what he might do, and is destined to do.*

In a totalitarian state, this is taken even further though by the sheer arbitrariness of the arrests and charges and punishments: the Minority Report *meets* The Purge.

 A totalitarian regime is not actually a government in the traditional sense, so to expect it to act like one would be a mistake. Look at it as a movement instead, and it becomes much more understandable and predictable.

If it makes anyone feel better, wannabe dictators like Trump, are just that: wannabe dictators. Their ambition and scope are limited. All they want is direct power to manifest their limited agenda in their home country.

Totalitarian rulers, on the other hand, have a larger agenda and power dynamic in mind. They are looking long-term at global conquest. They usually have some kind of ideological vehicle that fuels their overall purpose.

A country ruled by a dictator can live within a community of nations, however imperfectly. The dictatorship can also end with the death of the dictator. A totalitarian rule looks at other nations as snacks along the way to total global domination. It cannot help it; it is integral to its DNA.

While it may have been started by a charismatic leader, it can outlive such a leader because it is driven by an overarching ideology, independent of individual leaders.

⊛ *To a totalitarian state, material loss in terms of manpower, land, industrial and economic capacities, etc., are not true losses, but rather incidental sacrifices to a greater goal.*

Looking at such losses without understanding the true motive and driving intent, will only lead to a miscalculation of possible outcomes and possible responses. Focus should be on the ideological component of each decision of a totalitarian state.

⊛ *A totalitarian regime is always on the lookout for new enemies each time it eliminates old ones. It must keep the fiction of its purpose alive, while it kills.*

⊛ *Authority is not necessarily a bad thing. In any organization, especially a hierarchal one. Authority is needed to direct and utilize people and resources to get things done and accomplish organizational goals.*

This necessarily restricts people's individual freedoms, as their labour and talents are slaved together towards a higher organizational purpose. But this individual constraint frees the organization to maximize its potential.

But a totalitarian state is not interested in maximizing either people's or an organization's power to achieve anything. A totalitarian state's determination is to destroy freedom at all levels. Crushing people's souls is not too strong a description of its intent.

⊛ *All ideologies have one thing in common: they want to change human nature. They want to impose their particular ideology, their particular definition of humanity, on everyone. Because not everyone will agree with them, the only way to do this is by force.*

The 'efficiencies' some see in totalitarian regimes is misleading. The basic, inherent paranoia of such regimes demands such close monitoring of its population and each stage of government, and all its personnel, it, by default, creates a second shadow government duplicating the first, and actually having ultimate authority over it.

True power emanates from the Party. Efficiency is not the intent. This shadow government, while duplicating government functions, wants the non-structure of the original driving movement to maintain its ability to move as needed, to morph as needed, unhindered by formal structure. Other shadow forms may also exist. They tend to proliferate.

In a totalitarian state, everyone is a suspect. There are no innocents. Purges happen on a regular, yet unpredictable basis.

To understand a totalitarian state, how it uses power will give a better understanding than looking at it from its obvious organizational structure.

The apparent organizational structure was created to obfuscate the state's true purpose and intentions, and to hide those with true power. As Hannah Arendt observed: 'Real power begins where secrecy begins.'

Power, by its very nature, does not want permanent structures. At times, it does manifest itself in order to accomplish a particular task, but once done, power reverts back to its preferred, formless state.

Sometimes, the structure power will inhabit is that of a person. But that person is also only a temporary receptacle.

In Christian theology, God forgives all sins if only the sinner would just repent and ask for forgiveness.

But when God, in looking at the annihilation camps of history, recoiled in incomprehensible horror, He looked to His own Creator to explain such total evil.

Totalitarian thought, given actualized power, leads to what even God cannot comprehend from His own creations.

Man is left seeking remedies that do not exist. It is as if Man finds an alien species in its midst, one that does not conform to any historical or established norms, and does not know what to make of this species, or what to do with it.

Confusion also arises because of the alien species uncanny resemblance to humans. Can human institutions, laws, and norms apply to this new species? If not, what is to be done?

In a totalitarian regime there is a rush for ideology to replace common sense.

The differences between Party and State in a totalitarian regime should be closely monitored.

They are usually not the same. The Party represents the movement (whatever that may be). The State represents the functions of the government.

The Party floats above the State, distinct, separate, immune from the State's particular laws and regulations. The Party's own 'laws' are arbitrary and enforced without due process, even against the State.

Power. Look to the source of power. A government, a movement, derives its power from somewhere. Look beyond the obvious.

Unfettered laissez faire *capitalism** views the world and everything in it in terms of profit and loss, including human beings.

Such a viewpoint cannot help but find many people superfluous to its needs. We see this in the homeless, the stateless, the many unemployed and underemployed.

Capitalism gobbles up everything till there is nothing left, destroying along the way. Left unfettered, it cannot help it. In its own way, capitalism is a totalitarian ideology.

So, as in nature, it needs an opposing force, or forces, to help keep it in check. The free marketplace, via competition, does this only sporadically and, left to itself, not very effectively.

This is where government has a role. The extent of this role can be debated, but only a true zealot, or a blind person, can deny this need for some government oversight.

But this capitalistic ecology viewpoint has also infected the overall society. People just assume this is the only way to structure a society.

Of course, we have all seen the benefits of capitalism, but looking at the world and all its people, from such a limited, utilitarian point of view, can have dire unforeseen consequences for the entire planet.

Newness and creativity are lethal to any ideology. Their internal truth demands that their truth, their way, is sufficient, and all that is needed.

Anything new threatens this world-view. It cannot be tolerated. Given the power, ideologies will destroy what they feel threatens them, regardless of the consequences.

Against any ideology, common sense and facts can find no purchase. Ideologies are surrounded by an impervious union of true belief and contempt for reality.

Ideologies become dangerous when they reach a critical mass in numbers and sometimes with the arrival of a charismatic leader.

Expansion of any ideology comes from its own internal logic, that its way is the only way. Not expanding would deny its truth.

It is when police action, military action, is purposely taken against innocents that we know we have entered into the realm of the absurd, necessary for any atrocity to be contemplated.

In the 'land of the free and home of the brave', *why does the US imprison so many of its people and have so many prisons?*

Although the US makes up about 4.2 percent of the world's population, it accounts for 20 percent of the world's prison population (2023).

The US is out of line not only with its developed peers but also with authoritarian nations like Cuba, Russia, and China. The United States has the largest known prison population in the world (1.8 million people as of 2023).

Does the US have so many bad people? So many bad laws? The US even has its own small concentration camp at Guantanamo Bay detention center, holding prisoners without formal charge and with no legal rights. They are called 'alleged enemy combatants'.

They are held in a legal and political limbo. Overall, the 'land of the free and home of the brave' *needs to look closely at itself. What does all this say about the United States?*

It seems that many times the courts are basing their judgements on what political winds are pushing them, rather than on sound principles and standards, that can be applied across the board, regardless of the status of the offender.

Mixing, equating, criminals or criminal behaviour, with innocents, as in the case of immigrants, makes it possible to talk about doing, or even to do, the worst things imaginable to them.

Immigrants, whose only crime is to try and seek a better life, are now categorized as common criminals, and treated accordingly.

This viewpoint, also seeping into the general population, makes such treatment deservedly normal and warranted. After all, they must deserve it, otherwise it would not happen to them.

People crave to belong. They cannot stand isolation. So, even when arbitrarily placed into a subjective category, they will cling to this category, extolling its virtues above others, even as their own category is subjected to non-judicial horrors. They will tolerate this because there are other categories they perceive as lower than their own, and within their own category, they are not alone, they have an identity, they belong.

Once a totalitarian movement has gained power, the only thing preventing it from completing its mission, the total subjugation of humankind according to its ruling ideology, is the very people in power.

They are human. They have human 'inefficiencies'. They have human needs and wants. They live and die. Their very own hierarchy of needs demands individual action and fulfillment.

So, within the totalitarian machine, human cogs gum up the works. This is a good thing.

Look around the world, even in your own backyard, and you will see a new category of criminal manifesting itself all over. This category is determined simply by the 'crime' of 'being'. Being something 'other'. Being stateless, being homeless, being foreign, being weak, being different.

No actual crime needs to have been done. Just being, whatever. It is why they were born. To be a victim. To be victimized. Eventually, to be exterminated.

When it is finally time to die (be killed) in a totalitarian regime, the victim (always a victim), despite his animal-self fighting it strenuously to the end, knows rationally that death is the best thing that could happen to him.

No longer will he have an opportunity to betray his own family and friends, or even betray his own self, his own humanity. Death is a blessing.

This is the existence many blind idiots pursue. This is the utopia, where their truth and justice will prevail.

All totalitarian states end up this way, regardless of the initial ideology pursued. It is part of their very DNA, which cannot be denied.

The very laws in a democracy that make all people equal before the law, need to be carefully monitored. For it is precisely this 'equality' that deprives us all of our individuality; itself, a cornerstone of democracy.

⬦ *The behaviour and treatment of prisoners in a concentration camp in totalitarian regimes, is just a testing ground.*

The idea is to make the camps themselves superfluous, obsolete. The intent, eventually, is to make the whole country just one gigantic camp, replete with all its arbitrary capricious horrors, and punishments, such that total subjugation and control of the entire population is achieved.

⬦ *Part of the strength of the far-right is how easily its lies are picked up by its believers and supporters and spewed back out without needing any sort of formal coordination or fact-checking.*

The fact that a lie may change or morph into something different from the initial lie is only seen as a benefit. It adds further confusion to a message that was intended to do that anyway.

Members of the United States' Congress, and others, who have openly supported Trump and his Big Lie, who have attempted a takeover of the Capital on Jan 6th, have indeed burned their metaphorical bridges behind them into the fast-moving currents of truth and reality, that now cannot be repaired.

If they go further, as Trump has agitated for, they will be so far beyond the pale that this will only increase their motivation to destroy their enemies (who is everyone not on their side).

'No going back' is emblazoned on their foreheads, because going back will mean facing the criminal justice system for their crimes.

Since the totalitarian regime can never be wrong, it follows that any future mistakes must be intentional sabotage.

A totalitarian movement or regime is hampered by the fact that it is insane. It can blindly ignore reality if that reality does not conform or support its own ideology. But eventually, reality always trumps delusion.

However, during its existence it can still cause tremendous damage. In fact, given a choice, it would destroy the world rather than admit defeat. It is insane, after all.

Some may think that they have entered into a version of 1984, complete with Big Brother and his ever-watching Eye. As when a totalitarian regime takes power, there is such a thing as a 'thought crime', where merely thinking, having doubts, about the Party line can be considered a crime sufficient for formal punishment. Thought crimes are automatically assumed. Still, strangely, 'thought crimes' are always eventually, self-confessed,

○ *Conspiracy theorists believe in the most unbelievable things (a Flat-Earth, Fake-Moon Landing, the Illuminati, Lizard People, etc., the list goes on), but they become political and worrisome when their numbers swell and they view the cause behind the theories as aspects of the government lying and hiding their nefarious activities and agendas.*

The conspiracists' almost obsessive accumulation of 'evidence' to support their claims is almost endearing, till they apply violence to try to counter what they think is some sort of plot against them, others, and the country.

○ *Some people, rather than believe that* 'shit sometimes just happens', *would rather see a conspiracy behind every calamity.*

The shaping of the world by hidden, sinister forces, orchestrated against all good, hardworking peoples, is for some not some fantastic, weird, crazy, far-out, conspiracy theory.

No, it is just common sense as this explanation fits all the facts. The 'facts' obtained by a closed-off world-view where information from outside sources is usually not even seen or heard, but even if it is, is seen as alien propaganda, that they are too intelligent to fall for.

All their information sources also tell them that they are correct in their thinking. Why would they believe strangers, outsiders? That defies common sense.

For many of the MAGA-right, the distinction between true and false, fact and fiction, right and wrong, no longer has any connection or actual link to reality. Instead, they follow a self-interest-based blind faith in a person or religion that has no connection or link to reality either.

In a totalitarian regime, the role of the police has become much simpler to implement: everyone is guilty.

Mass purges, so common in totalitarian states, seem to follow the ancient Chinese system of degrees of responsibility for any serious crime.

If someone has irked the emperor for some reason, he and his family will be killed to certain degrees, say to three or four degrees. Nine degrees was considered extreme.

What this means is that anyone connected by blood to the person charged, even faintly, as degrees enlarge, is killed for the crime the original individual may have done.

The totalitarian state has gone even further. The connections to the original 'criminal' are no longer just determined by bloodline, but includes anyone even remotely connected, even complete strangers, who might have had the misfortune to have crossed paths with someone known to someone, known to someone, known to...it goes on and on, with some obscure, tenuous, link back to th original nexus.

Countless people can be swept up in such purges, made even easier today with computers.

The end result being that even the memories of people's former existence is wiped out. There is no one left to remember. That is the intent.

To give something a name, then place an 'ism' at the end of it, should be resisted. It gives the so named a power and respect it may not deserve or be warranted. It seems to imply the ponderous, legitimizing weight of authority and scholarship behind it.

People wonder why anyone would voluntarily go to such countries as Russia, North Korea, Iran, countries of such ilk, countries that are basically dictatorships?

They may think that they are safe because they are innocent of any illegal intent. They are tourists, they are there for business reasons, there to perhaps visit extended family, all valid, honest reasons.

What they do not seem to understand is that dictatorial regimes, consider all outsiders, all foreigners, as spies for their home governments. After all, if their own citizens travel abroad, they automatically go as spies in addition to any other ostensible purpose.

So, if these innocent visitors to state dictatorships, get detained, arrested, their guilt is already assumed. Any professing of innocence is automatically dismissed. Any 'proof' of innocence is assumed to be fabricated. Truths are lies. There is no 'truth'.

It is a way of life and thinking, that strangely enough, allows them to believe anything and nothing. Outsiders have a hard time comprehending this.

In a dictatorship the tyranny of the masses is enforced from outside. This is no longer needed in totalitarian rule, as the people, in psychological isolation, tyrannize themselves into submission.

There is no consolation in saying that everything has an end, even the most ruthless dictatorships of totalitarian regimes, if that end embodies also the end of human civilization, or even the species.

Looking back at the records and memories of totalitarian states, and attempting to understand them and their reality, truth can no longer be seen as the ultimate arbitrator of reality. Nor can natural consequences, as totalitarian states seem to do things that go against perceived common sense and good judgement.

Truth and reality can only be defined after the fact. By that time damage has already been done. Whomever is looking back then, trying to understand, is severely handicapped by lack of direct experience and limited information, and their own personal and cultural filters.

Truth becomes an opinion and an empty debate. Truth is seen as only propaganda for a particular viewpoint. The past is already unreal, and continuously slips away each and every day, as does truth.

In totalitarian regimes, the concept that 'everything is possible', will not take you to the stars, but to mass extermination and concentration camps.

When national borders became solidified, it left those peoples who had yet to declare themselves, (or could not), this-or-that, at a loss as to their official identity, and left them exposed as 'foreigners' in their own land.

Even in Europe, this can be seen, where currently there are about 500,000 stateless people. This becomes important in peoples' self-identification as to who they are, how they identify themselves, and also, how they are legally defined.

The corresponding rise in neo-tribalism of some Americans indicates that these people identify more with some mythical, ideal, pure, ethnic identity than with the country they currently live in, and are citizens of.

They are choosing this neo-tribal identity over their identity with any particular country, including America. If they also decide to become 'stateless', this can have profound implications in terms of national identity, patriotism, and national unity.

People now move and operate in a world that many, if not most, do not understand. Our technology, and its potential consequences, escape our limited comprehension.

Even scientists and technologists usually know and understand only portions of their own creations, and certainly know nothing of their future impacts and interactions. The rest of us, know even less.

The majority of people now seem to be mindless masses going about their daily lives oblivious to how the world now actually operates, their own artificial one, or the natural one.

Yet, people still have to make political decisions. Who to vote for, why this candidate and not another? Are their campaign promises real, accurate? How would anyone know? Especially when issues deal with things that affect us all, that have dire consequences if we get it wrong.

We have to trust someone with our votes. But who? Perhaps this is why so many people do not vote. Are not politically active, as they see no link between politics and their regular, daily lives, their ongoing struggle just to live.

But politics is important. Things political, decided at local, state, or national levels, do affect everyone, from local book banning, to climate change.

They affect us all. If people do not get involved, the ongoing experiment in democracy may just fail.

The world is spinning out of control, and when it finally spins off the edge, all that will be left are the old known standards of war, famine, disease, destruction. We do not have to accept this fate.

We do have the power to affect positive change. We, each of us.

Politics has to do with people and their shared interactions. So, when there is a cry in society for 'people' to do something, to correct some problem, forgotten is that 'people' is made up of individuals. There are no 'people', as such.

Action must, and can only start and be maintained, by each and every individual. The individual must vote. The individual must show up and march. The individual must attend town hall meetings.

Of course, people in concert can achieve great things, but that group, that team, that crowd, is made up of individual people..

With all the vast powers and wealth that some conspiracy theorists bestow on these Grand Conspirators who secretly control the world, you would think that these Grand Conspirators would do a better job?

The world usually seems to be in a mess. But no, even those failures fit into the conspiracy theorist's world-view. All these failures all over the world and throughout history are just to screen the true intentions and hide the true manipulations going on out of sight. It's a self-fulfilling logic with no end.

With that said, however, it does not mean that there are no conspiracies. There are, just not that comprehensive or coordinated.

There are many much smaller, relatively speaking, conspiracies. Sometimes they overlap, intentionally or not. But their intentions are still veiled in mystery. But, also, some show up in the most illuminating ways.

The politics of people depends on talking to each other, in communicating each other's thoughts, needs, and opinions. Talking to each other is political engagement, and as people are political animals, this is a good thing. Disengagement from the body politic is a dangerous passivity that can only have negative consequences for everyone and the overall society.

The human animal, barely out of the cave, has now smashed the atom, has created a world-spanning civilization, has developed advanced AI, has now ventured out into space - taking its neurosis with it. It lives in a high-tech society no one really comprehends, and yet, despite all this, this human animal does not grasp or understand its own basic human nature or predicament.

This human animal has unleashed forces, tangible and intangible, that it many times does not fully understand or is not even aware that they exist. It acts like it is still living in the cave, with its simple pleasures, needs, and responsibilities, with little understanding that the fire it so recently discovered, can burn as well as provide needed warmth.

The ability, and just pure need to think, think about life, its purpose, about the human condition, is not meant to be left only to social scientists or philosophers. When people think, talk, and share, things get done.

It does not matter what the action is, what the behaviour is, what the motive is - perhaps even nefarious in the extreme - as long as the original command falls under the colour, the guise, of 'official acts'; therefore, immunity takes place.

Does this make sense to anyone? Does it only take Supreme Court Justices, with their elevated minds, to fail to see what is readily apparent to all others, that this is pure, dangerous nonsense?

Immigration has become such an important, contentious issue in this country, it has risen to the level of becoming very decisive in our next presidential election.

Some of this issue is just hype, with no reliance on truth or facts. But it is true, though, that the American immigration system has been in dire need for reform for decades.

When new immigrants come to this country, the expectation is that they will assimilate, become Americans. But how is this assimilation defined?

Is it based on assimilation of national principles within the immigrant population, like belief in the American constitution, the rule of law, gender equality, etc.; or, is it based on the assimilation of national identity, where the immigrant totally gives up their former national and cultural identity, to fully absorb American ways, norms, language, and culture?

Melting pot or salad bowl? Which is better? America has thrived on both. Why force a choice at all, since both seem to work so well? But integration has always been a multigenerational process, so full assimilation can take time.

But immigration has become such a fractious issue politically and culturally in this country, it is past time the United States improve its immigration system and policies.

This can also only help to improve immigration's image as not a problem, but an ongoing asset for the country, which it actually is.

Some countries, like Canada, for instance, have a Comprehensive Ranking System, of some sort, where new potential immigrants are 'ranked', based on established, agreed upon, criteria for entry into the country, such as: skills, education, language ability, work experience, financial status, etc. These criteria when used to rank potential immigrants, can only help with the process of eventual immigrant assimilation, smoothing the way for a full integration into American society, with as few bumps as possible.

As the United States birth rate is falling, as it is in most developed countries, immigration, as in the past, but now with a new urgency, provides a new and vibrant, and much needed source of innovative and fresh blood for the economy and the country.

Keep in mind, that one in four Americans today is either an immigrant or a child of one. Immigration is not new to America; it just needs to work better for both native-born and new arrivals.

It has been long said that Man is a political animal, sometimes implying a negative. This is true. Man as a social creature, cannot help but become engaged in politics any time he shares space and engages with another human being. This is so basic that its importance is so easily overlooked. People must consciously become political. Must stay political.

The politics of being in this world is of vital importance to Humanity's welfare on this planet, if not to the planet itself.

One of the first things a dictator or a totalitarian regime does, is to close its borders - both ways.

Power and helplessness — both paradoxical feelings shared in common by all people, more often in today's world.

We have all seen, on a daily basis, how the MAGA-right continues to lie. Lie about everything, even if on the surface the lie seems stupid, obvious, even counterproductive.

Yet, they continue to do it. Fact checking has failed. There are just too many lies. It is called lie-swamping, overloading the system till it becomes non-functional.

What we have also seen on a daily basis is how the main-stream media just no longer seems to care. It just accepts the lies. At times, it may comment on some obvious lies, but it has given up any meaningful pushback.

It seems the constant barrage of lies has fulfilled its function. Many who listen to the news can now no longer tell what is true or not.

Of course, we could always just assume that when the MAGA-right speak, they are automatically lying. This could work, but many of the lies have percolated through social media and society without people being aware of their source.

But it certainly would help if the mainstream media would not just blindly accept any pronouncements made by the MAGA-right.

Do not just ask a question, receive an answer (any answer), then go on to the next question on a list, all without thought or question, just to get through the interview, saying you have fulfilled your responsibility to 'fairly' hear both sides of an issue.

In a free society, the Media must function properly. It must do its job. Many times, it is the only source that has access to those in power. It needs to fulfill its responsibility as a crucial pillar of a free society, otherwise its last free headline might be:
AMERICA FUBAR!

AMERICA:

FUBAR!

VOTE

UNIVERSAL HUMAN RIGHTS & DUTIES

The following UNIVERSAL HUMAN RIGHTS & DUTIES is an attempt to create and formulate a consensual, yet, necessarily simple in format, charter, that can be applied across a wide variety of dispersed, non-homogenized, Human nations, societies, cultures, and peoples.

At this point in time, this charter is more a fantasy than a reality, yet considering the current world situation with rampant war, famines, widespread diseases, increasing mass migrations, and the looming threat of climate change, it was felt that an attempt to formulate something simple, yet doable (?), is not only needed, necessary, but crucial to the actual survival of our global civilization, if not our species.

Many sources, and authors (including Professor Nalangu, who is a contributing author to this project), were used to create this charter. Some sources are listed at the end, but in particular: A SYSTEMATIC THEORY OF UNIVERSAL ETHICS AND A CODE FOR GLOBAL MORAL EDUCATION, by Enno A. Winkler MD PhD (2022), was used as a framework. It is simple in structure, yet captures what needs to be said and done. The simplicity may rest in that it had a single author, and was not written by a committee.

We all hope that in reading this, you can find something that resonates within you, and can motivate you to promote this, or something akin to it, to your respective political representatives.

It is recognized that this manifesto is incomplete, particularly in the ENFORCEMENT section, as is common in many of the listed sources; for example, in the Geneva Conventions on the Rules of Engagement in war.

UNIVERSAL HUMAN RIGHTS & DUTIES
Guiding Principles

This UNIVERSAL HUMAN RIGHTS & DUTIES is an attempt to create and formulate a consensual, yet, necessarily simple in format, charter, that can be applied across a wide variety of dispersed, non-homogenized, Human nations, societies, cultures, and peoples.

Human caused extinction may be avoided if Humanity will be willing to accept basic rules of common conduct.

UNIVERSAL HUMAN RIGHTS & DUTIES binds all people collectively and each one separately.

Commandments

(1) Respect the other as yourself.
(2) Respect the truth.
(3) Do not steal.
(4) Respect life.
(5) Protect nature.

Principles

1) Each human being is endowed with personal dignity (dignity is the right of a person to be valued and respected for their own sake, and to be treated ethically. The Golden Rule, the Rule of Reciprocity, or Kant's Categorical Imperative, come to mind as basic examples).

2) An individual's liberty finds its limits where the dignity of the other begins.

3) State, religious, economic, and other office holders are in service to the individual.

4) Human aspirations for progress can only be realized by agreed values and standards applying to all people and institutions at all times.

5) The rational actor model, must cease being the basis for political and social policy. Making the various populations feel like they belong to the greater group, may be the single best long-term strategy for reducing conflict and war: building cohesive societies stops both internal violence and intergroup conflict.

6) The antidote to polarization comes from overlapping group membership and loyalties.

7) Policies that distribute the pie more widely should lead to more balanced power in society, and edge societies towards peace.

8) Peace is not just an absence of war. It is a positive activity. Active peace can be defined as the availability or provision of food, shelter, health, education, and justice, as well as freedom and human dignity. If these things can be provided for, or made available, to all and any peoples, then war, itself, becomes the outlier, not the expected norm. Governments, nations, peoples, should be looking at their own societies to see where they fall short on these attributes of active peace, and fill the gaps where needed. They then should also look outside their own borders to promote an active peace in those societies that lack this foundation. *It will be discovered that a truly comprehensive active peace cannot be found anywhere if it is lacking somewhere.* Peace is not just a given. Peace cannot be assumed to be the base state for all humans, forever. Peace must be pursued and fought for, on many fronts. This is not an oxymoron; it is a basic truth.

9) The freedom of indifference is not acceptable to a humane, progressive society. History has repeatedly warned that freedom without involvement and acceptance of responsibility can destroy the freedom itself; whereas, when rights and responsibilities are balanced, then freedom is enhanced and a better world can be created.

10) When power is unequal, unaccountable, and centralized, a society is left vulnerable to the whims and private interests of rulers and elites. This must be recognized and accounted for.

11) The more freedom we enjoy, as a society and as individuals, the greater the responsibility we bare, toward others as well as ourselves.

12) We have a duty and responsibility to protect and promote a safe, stable and healthy environment, promoting respect, protection, and preservation of the uniqueness and diversity of all forms of life. To promote an adequate use of resources avoiding excessive exploitation and consumption.

13) Sovereignty is not absolute. In a recognized *'league of nations'*, full sovereignty is recognized as not being absolute. Certain rights, duties, obligations are seen as *'international'* in scope. In a Democracy, if all Rights devolve to the individual, the individual must then have a means to protect those Rights if the Law cannot or refuses to do so, otherwise those Rights become meaningless.

14) Many people have asked, and many governments, and organizations, have disputed us on this issue, but the question is: *Why is so much emphasis placed on the individual?* The reason is that, if you look

closely at the prior *Principles*, it will be noticed that most mention and require that the individual is crucial and central to the accomplishment of the Human Rights & Duties listed. Our perspective is that the individual is the foundation upon which all societies depend and function. Nothing would exist without the individual. This journey, this search, for a principled, coherent, just society, begins and ends with the individual; hence, the individual's importance in this schema.

Enforcement

The violation of these principles and commandments is subject to social rejection and punishment under equal rules and laws for everyone.

The importance of the concept of self-responsibility towards attaining the self-realization of these listed *Principles* cannot be overlooked or overstated. Unless each individual is involved in the creation, accomplishment is diminished, or even may be impossible, certainly more difficult.

This section is based, in part, on:

The Magna Carta (1215)

The United States of America's Declaration of
Independence (1776)

The United States Constitution (1787)

France's Declaration of the Rights of Man
and of the Citizen (1789)

THE UNIVERSAL DECLARATION OF
HUMAN RIGHTS (1948)

UNIVERSAL DECLARATION OF HUMAN
RESPONSIBILITIES (1997)

EARTH CHARTER (2000)

MILLENIUM DEVELOPMENT GOALS (2000)

RESPONSIBILITY TO PROTECT (2005)

THE 2030 AGENDA FOR SUSTAINABLE
DEVELOPMENT (2015)

A SYSTEMATIC THEORY OF UNIVERSAL
ETHICS AND A CODE FOR GLOBAL MORAL
EDUCATION
By Enno A. Winkler MD PhD (2022)

(All worthwhile reads.)

SOS

*Never have we depended so much on political
forces that cannot be trusted to follow the
rules of common sense.*
~ Hannah Arendt

*When they call the roll in the Senate, the
Senators do not know whether to answer
'Present' or 'Not Guilty'.*
— Theodore Roosevelt

*We easily recognize the Evil Empire in the movies,
but it is harder to see it in the mirror.*
~ Santiago Bardo

*In politics, many praise freedom,
but demand security.*
~ Tristan Graeme Ash

*Unlimited power in the hands of limited
people always leads to cruelty.*
~ Aleksandr Solzhenitsyn

*Just as the poet is a menace to conformity,
he is also a constant threat to political dictators.*
~ Rollo May

*I have found that, to make a contented slave,
it is necessary to make a thoughtless one.*
~ Frederick Douglass

*Ambition must be made to counteract ambition.
The interest of the man must be connected with the
constitutional rights of the place.*
~ James Madison

God is not coming.
~ Jamie Glasgow

STUFF

Lucy Nalangu Bio.

Teacher, writer, social activist, social scientist, political philosopher, formerly Professor of Law, History & Moral Philosophy at the University of Nairobi, previously taught at the University of Oxford, UK, and Harvard University, US. Currently, is a freelance researcher, professional writer, commentator, and consultant.

James Sawers Bio.

James Sawers is a citizen of the United States of America, having emigrated from the United Kingdom at an early age. He has a bachelor's degree in psychology, and a master's in management. He is a sandan in the Japanese martial art of aikido.

He is also a veteran, a former paratrooper with the 82nd Airborne Division (*All the Way!*): 2/504 (*Devils in Baggy Pants*) & 2/508 (*Death from Above*). A former member of the 2nd Infantry Division (Indianhead) (*Second to None!*) - ROK/U.S. Combined Division; 2nd Battalion, 9th Infantry Regiment (Mechanized) (*Keep Up the Fire!*) "Manchu" (Imjin Scouts).

Definitions

Moral Philosophy

Character List

Nation, Nation-State, State,
Sovereign State,
Country

Socialism

Communism

Capitalism

Democratic Socialism

Democracy

Liberalism

Libertarianism

Totalitarianism

Administrative State

Despot/Dictator

Moral Philosophy

Moral philosophy is the branch of philosophy that contemplates what is right and wrong. It explores the nature of morality and examines how people should live their lives in relation to others.

Moral philosophy has three branches.

One branch, meta-ethics, investigates big picture questions such as, "What is morality?" "What is justice?" "Is there truth?" and "How can I justify my beliefs as better than conflicting beliefs held by others?"

Another branch of moral philosophy is normative ethics. It answers the question of what we ought to do. Normative ethics focuses on providing a framework for deciding what is right and wrong. Three common frameworks are deontology, utilitarianism, and virtue ethics.

The last branch is applied ethics. It addresses specific, practical issues of moral importance such as war and capital punishment. Applied ethics also tackles specific moral challenges that people face daily, such as whether they should lie to help a friend or co-worker.

(Wikipedia)

Character List

For simplicities sake, particular definitions used in this book parallel, and are guided by, those of Hannah Arendt, from her book: *The Origins of Totalitarianism*, However, any changes, deviations, are this author's *'mistakes'*.

The People

The *People* are the citizens of a nation-state. They are the people who work. They form the body politic and are the ultimate source of authority in the functioning nation-state. They are often mistaken for the Mob or the Masses, both of which are degenerations of the People. In the mid-19th century, the People get split into classes, allowing for the Mob and the Masses to make their appearance.

The Mob

The *Mob* consists of the refuse of all classes of society. They search for a strong-man or great leader to follow. They always use extra-parliamentary (and often violent) means to accomplish political goals since they are not represented by parties that are based on the classes they have been ejected from. The Mob also plays a role in imperialism.

The Masses

The *Masses* refers to the mass of isolated, atomized individuals that is created by the destruction of the nation-state and the accumulation of capital during imperialism. The Masses are not the same as the Mob.

While the Mob is the refuse of all classes, the Masses are created by the apparent liquidation of classes. The Masses are the basis of totalitarian movements, which rely on a mass of humans who have lost all relations to their fellow man.

The Totalitarian Leader

The Totalitarian Leader is typified by Hitler and Stalin. The will of the Totalitarian Leader is the supreme law in a totalitarian regime, and all those who carry out this *supreme law* view themselves as merely instruments of the Leader's will and ideology rather than autonomous individuals making choices. The Totalitarian Leader is incredibly famous and charismatic, but will be forgotten immediately when he dies. Furthermore, he is the source of the *infallible predictions* so characteristic of totalitarian propaganda.

From: GradeSaver; Summary of *The Origins of Totalitarianism*, by Hannah Arendt; Character List.

Nation, Nation-State, State, Sovereign State, Country

Nation is a large body of people united by common origin, history, culture, ethnicity, or language. The main difference between *State* and *Nation* is that State is a political and legal entity whereas Nation is a socio-cultural entity. A State is a territory considered as an organized political community under one government.

A **State** is a territorial entity, with a permanent population, defined borders, and a government that effectively controls the territory. States in which the overwhelming majority of people belong to one nation are known as **Nation-States.**

State, Nation, and *Country* are all terms that describe groups of people who live in the same place and have a great deal in common. But while **States** and **Sovereign States** are political entities, **Nations** and **Countries** might or might not be. A **Sovereign State** (sometimes called an Independent State) has the following qualities:

1. A **State** is a territory with its own institutions and populations.
2. A **Nation** is a large group of people who inhabit a specific territory and are connected by history, culture, or another commonality.
   Nation is also a large body of people united by common origin, history, culture, ethnicity, or language. The main difference between **State** and **Nation** is that State is a political and legal entity

whereas Nation is a socio-cultural entity. A State is a territory considered as an organized political community under one government.

3. A **Nation-State** is a cultural group (a Nation) that is also a State (and may, in addition, be a **Sovereign State).**

4. The word **Country** can be used to mean the same thing as **State, Sovereign State**, or **Nation-State**. It can also be used in a less political manner to refer to a region or cultural area that has no governmental status. Examples include Wine Country (the grape-growing area of northern California) and Coal Country (the coal-mining region of Pennsylvania).

5. A **Sovereign State** is a state with its own institutions and populations that has a permanent population, territory, and government. It must also have the right and capacity to make treaties and other agreements with other States.

A **Sovereign State** (sometimes called an Independent State) also has the following qualities:

a) Space or territory that has internationally recognized boundaries

b) People who live there on an ongoing basis

c) Regulations governing foreign and domestic trade

d) The ability to issue legal tender that is recognized across boundaries

e) An internationally recognized government that provides public services and police power and has the right to make treaties, wage war, and take other actions on behalf of its people

f) Sovereignty, meaning that no other State should have power over the country's territory

~ Wikipedia; Various Sources

Socialism, Communism, Capitalism, Democratic Socialism, Democracy, Liberalism, Libertarianism, Totalitarianism, Administrative State, Despot/Dictator

SOCIALISM: The meaning of SOCIALISM is any of various egalitarian economic and political theories or movements advocating collective or governmental ownership and administration of the means of production and distribution of goods. Some people see socialism (in Marxist theory) as a transitional social state between the overthrow of capitalism and the realization of Communism.

COMMUNISM: Communism is a form of government most closely associated with the ideas of Karl Marx, which he outlined in The Communist Manifesto. Communism is based on the goal of eliminating socioeconomic class struggles by creating a classless society in which everyone shares the benefits of labor and the state controls all property and wealth.

CAPITALISM: Capitalism is an economic system in which private individuals or businesses own capital goods. At the same time, business owners employ workers who receive only wages; labor doesn't own the means of production but instead uses them on behalf of the owners of capital.

The production of goods and services under capitalism is based on supply and demand in the general market, also known as the market economy. This is in contrast to a planned economy or a command economy, in which prices are set through central planning.

Capitalism is essentially an economic system in which the means of production — factories, tools, machines, raw materials, etc.— are organized by one or more business owners, also known as capitalists. Capitalists then hire workers to operate the means of production in return for wages. Workers usually have no claim on the means of production or on the profits generated from their labor; these belong to the capitalists.

The purest form of capitalism is free-market or *laissez-faire* capitalism. Here, private individuals are unrestrained. They may determine where to invest, what to produce or sell, and at which prices to exchange goods and services. The *laissez-faire* marketplace operates without checks or controls. In general, *laissez-faire* capitalism is a policy of minimum governmental interference in the economic affairs of individuals and society. *Laissez-faire* is a political as well as an economic doctrine. The pervading theory of the 19th century was that individuals, pursuing their own desired ends, would thereby achieve the best results for the society of which they were part. The function of the state was to maintain order and security and to avoid interference with the initiative of individuals in pursuit of their own desired goals. But *laissez-faire* advocates nonetheless argued that government had an essential role in enforcing contracts as well as ensuring civil order. In the late 19th century, the acute changes caused by industrial growth and the adoption of mass production techniques proved the *laissez-faire* doctrine insufficient as a guiding philosophy. The wild extremes of the economy at this time, the rise of so-called robber barons, the rising economic and social inequalities also exposed the inherent weakness of such a philosophy. Still, in modern times, some people still advocate for this philosophy.

Today, most countries practice a mixed capitalist system that includes some degree of government regulation of business and some extent of public ownership of select industries.

<u>DEMOCRATIC SOCIALISM</u>: A political ideology that supports the establishment of a democratically run and decentralized form of socialist economy. Modern democratic socialists vary widely in their views of how a proper socialist economy should function, but all share the goal of abolishing capitalism. Democratic socialism is a variant of socialism where the government is organized by democracy. In short, it believes that social and economic decisions should be made by those whom they most affect. The combination of the two ideologies of democracy and socialism makes democratic socialism. Democratic socialists believe that both the economy and society should be run democratically—to meet public needs, not to make profits for a few. To achieve a more just society, many structures of the government and economy must be radically transformed through greater economic and social democracy so that ordinary citizens can participate in the many decisions that affect their lives. Democratic socialists do not want to create an all-powerful government bureaucracy, but at the same time do not want big corporate bureaucracies to control our society either.

<u>DEMOCRACY</u>: is a system of government in which state power is vested in the people or the general population of a state. Under a minimalist definition of democracy, rulers are elected through competitive elections while more expansive definitions link democracy to guarantees of civil liberties and human rights in addition to competitive elections. In a direct democracy, the people have the direct authority to deliberate and decide legislation. In a representative democracy, the people choose governing officials through elections to do so.

<u>LIBERALISM:</u> Is a political and moral philosophy based on the rights of the individual, liberty, consent of the governed, political equality, right to private property and equality before the law. Liberals espouse various and often mutually warring views depending on their understanding of these principles but generally support private property, market economies, individual rights (including civil rights and human rights), liberal democracy, secularism, rule of law, economic and political freedom, freedom of speech, freedom of the press, freedom of assembly, and freedom of religion, constitutional government and privacy rights. Liberalism is frequently cited as the dominant ideology of modern history.

<u>LIBERTARIANISM:</u> Libertarianism, is a political philosophy that takes individual liberty to be the primary political value. A political philosophy that advocates only minimal state intervention in the free market and the private lives of citizens. It may be understood as a form of liberalism, classical liberalism in particular, the political philosophy associated with the English philosophers John Locke and John Stuart Mill, the Scottish economist Adam Smith, and the American statesman Thomas Jefferson. Liberalism seeks to define and justify the legitimate powers of government in terms of certain natural or God-given individual rights. These rights include the rights to life, liberty, private property, freedom of speech and association, freedom of worship, government by consent, equality under the law, and moral autonomy (the ability to pursue one's own conception of happiness, or the 'good life'). The purpose of government, according to liberals, is to protect these and other individual rights, and in general liberals have contended that government power should be limited to that which is necessary to accomplish this task. Libertarians are classical liberals who strongly emphasize the individual right to liberty. They contend

that the scope and powers of government should be constrained so as to allow each individual as much freedom of action as is consistent with a like freedom for everyone else. Thus, they believe that individuals should be free to behave and to dispose of their property as they see fit, provided that their actions do not infringe on the equal freedom of others.

<u>TOTALITARIANISM:</u> Totalitarianism is a form of government that permits no individual freedom and that seeks to subordinate all aspects of individual life to the authority of the state. In the broadest sense, totalitarianism is characterized by strong central rule that attempts to control and direct all aspects of individual life through coercion and repression.

Totalitarianism is often distinguished from **dictatorship, despotism, or tyranny** by its supplanting of all political institutions with new ones and its sweeping away of all legal, social, and political traditions. Dictatorship and totalitarianism are often associated, but they are actually two separate phenomena. Dictatorship is a form of government in which the ruler has the power to govern without consent of those being governed. Totalitarian governments are those that exert total control over the governed; they regulate nearly every aspect of public and private behavior. Totalitarianism entails a political system where the state recognizes no limits to its authority, and it strives to regulate every aspect of public and private life wherever feasible. Totalitarian regimes stay in political power through all-encompassing propaganda campaigns (disseminated through the state-controlled mass media), a single party that is often marked by political repression, personality cultism, control over the economy, regulation and restriction of speech, mass surveillance, and widespread use of terror.

The totalitarian state pursues some special goal, such as class struggle, racial purity, usually via force and conquest, to the exclusion of all others. All resources are directed toward its attainment, regardless of the cost. Whatever might further the goal is supported; whatever might foil the goal is rejected. This obsession spawns an ideology that explains everything in terms of the goal, rationalizing all obstacles that may arise and all forces that may contend with the state. The resulting 'popular support' permits the state the widest latitude of action of any form of government. Any dissent is branded evil, and internal political differences are not permitted. Totalitarianism displays significant elements of traditional religion, such as rites of purgation, penitence and renewal, cultic patterns of behaviour, heresy, and obedience to an ultimate authority that cannot be questioned.

Because pursuit of the goal is the only ideological foundation for the totalitarian state, achievement of the goal can never be acknowledged, otherwise the state has lost its unifying, driving purpose, its very reason for existence. A totalitarian state is also recognized by its refusal to recognize traditional national boundaries. Its driving ideology, whatever it might be, demands a constant expansion. Total world domination is its ultimate goal. It also tends to view achievement of its objectives as a long-term struggle.

<u>ADMINISTRATIVE STATE</u>: is a term used to describe the power that some government agencies have to write, judge, and enforce their own laws. Since it pertains to the structure and function of government, it is a frequent topic in political science, constitutional law, and public administration. The administrative state is created when legislative (law-making) bodies, like the U.S. Congress or the U.K. Parliament, delegate their lawmaking powers to administrative or private entities, as in other government agencies, like the United States' EPA, for example. In recent years, in the U.S., some argue that the Administrative State runs counter to the U.S. Constitution. Some recent court cases reflect this argument. Some think that if the power of the Administrative State is cut down or severely diminished, the government will become paralyzed and will be unable to function effectively. Laws made by administrative agencies are typically distinguished from laws written by the legislature, and given a separate term like 'regulations' or 'rules', or referred to in codified form as 'codes'.

DESPOT: A ruler with absolute power and authority. One exercising power tyrannically (a tyrant is a usurper; one who gains power and rules extralegally, distinguished from kings elevated by election or succession): a person exercising absolute power in a brutal or oppressive way. A government by a singular authority, either a single person or tight-knit group, which rules with absolute power.

DICTATOR: A dictator is a political leader who possesses absolute power. A dictatorship is a state ruled by one dictator or by a small clique. The word originated as the title of a Roman dictator elected by the Roman Senate to rule the republic in times of emergency. Like the term tyrant, and to a lesser degree autocrat, dictator came to be used almost exclusively as a term for oppressive rule.

~ Wikipedia; Various Internet Sources

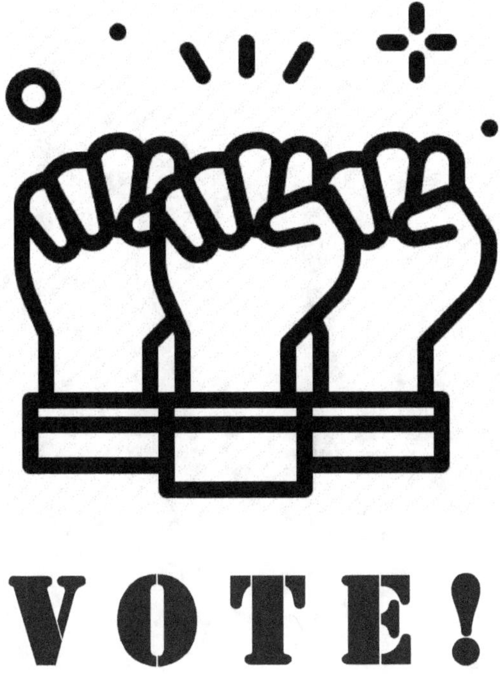
VOTE!

Immunity

Kings and queens
All seem to agree
That supreme immunity
Does not rest on ye
The people, the dirty masses
Always just sitting on their asses

It rests in the blood royale
Not far from the golden royal urinal
Cause they are so different
Born to rule and automatically be
The very best you will ever see

Even your mudsill Court
Calling itself Supreme – as if!
Saw in its *wisdom*
That some are born to rule
With immunity such a useful tool

You can kill whom you want
Without much of a thought
Cause everything is kosher
Even if you are not

But, alas, even the people
The lazy, downtrodden masses
Can no longer expect
Anonymity to cover their asses

Cause everyone is an enemy now
And a victim, too
As people try to hunker down
In this wonderful new zoo

But all that can be seen
Once all the gates are breached
On the naked shores of history
Even royalty is left beached

The corpses pile up and up
As the courts now rule
That anything is now possible
Nothing is too cruel

Welcome to America
Land of the free
Home of the brave
As immunity now chases us
All to the grave

~ June Cumberland

Veterans Crisis Hotline

VETERANS CRISIS HOTLINE

We're here anytime, day or night – 24/7

If you are a Veteran in crisis or concerned about one, connect with our caring, qualified responders for confidential help. Many of them are Veterans themselves.

- Call **988 and select 1**
- Text **838255**
- https://www.veteranscrisisline.net/get-help-now/chat/
- Call TTY if you have hearing loss
  - **800-799-4889**

or:
1-800-273-8255 and Press 1

Social Media Contact

If you want to hear more about James Sawers's upcoming books and works, or contact him, or join him on social media:

Facebook:

James Sawers
www.facebook.com/sawersX

Email: nothingwerks42@gmail.com

(The above methods are the ONLY way to contact the author.)